My name is

Brynn McKolosky.

red stop sign

STOP

blueberry pie

blue

hats

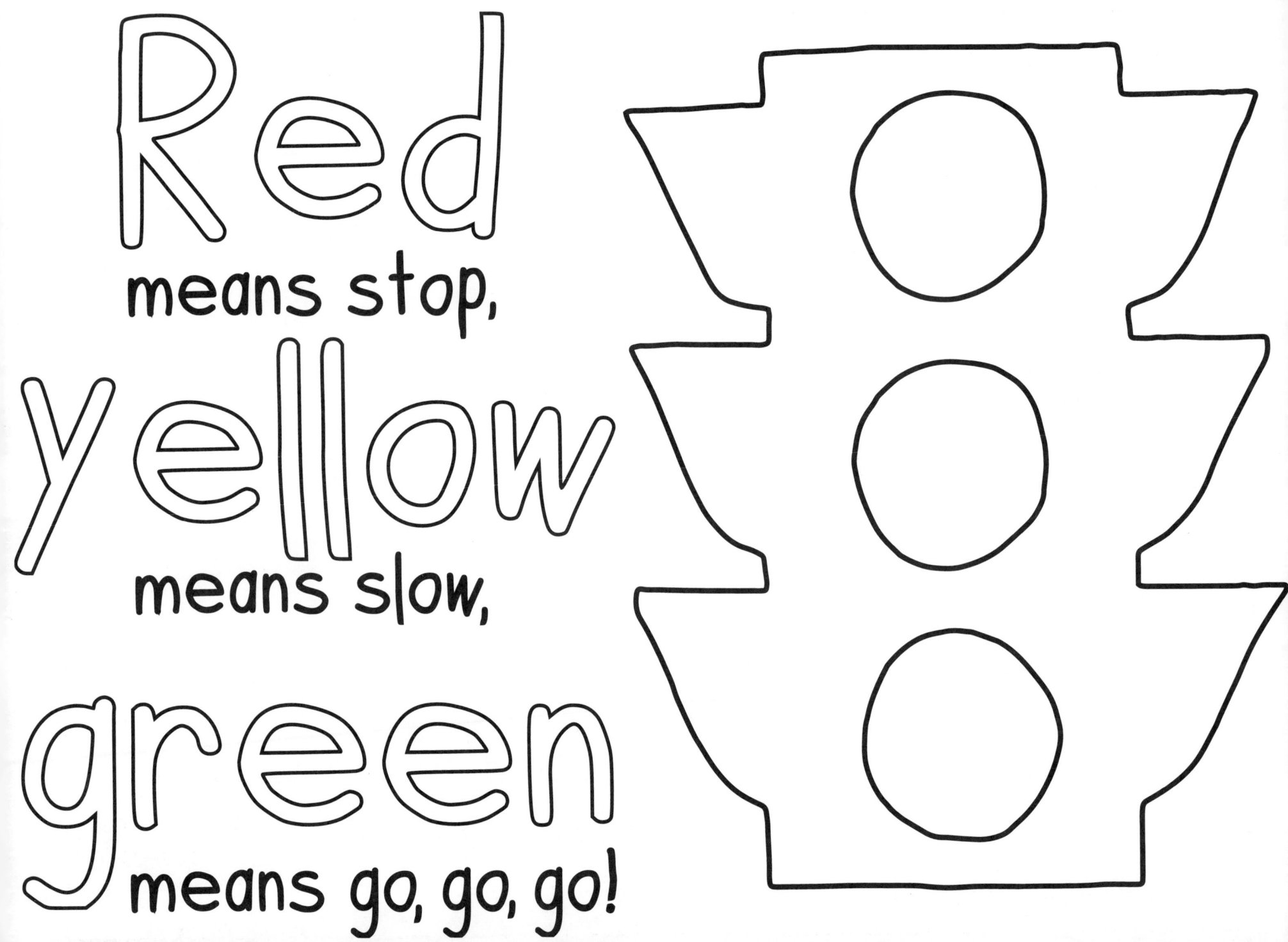

Traffic Light

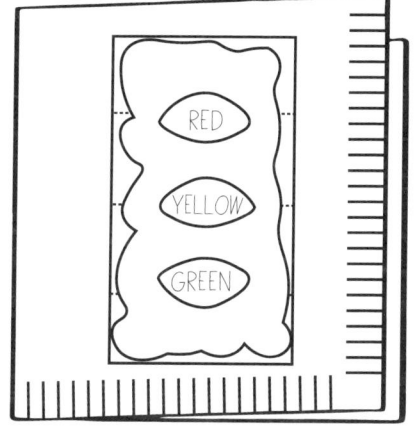

Color Rap Recipe

Supplies:
- Bag of red apples
- Bag of green apples
- Bag of yellow apples
- Jar of creamy peanut butter or other spreadable topping
- Box of graham crackers
- Package of napkins
- Package of utensils for spreading

Teacher preparations:
- Wash, slice the apples
- Separate apple slices by color
- If desired, toss the sliced apples with diluted lemon juice or lemon-lime soda to prevent browning.
- Arrange supplies near step-by-step direction cards.

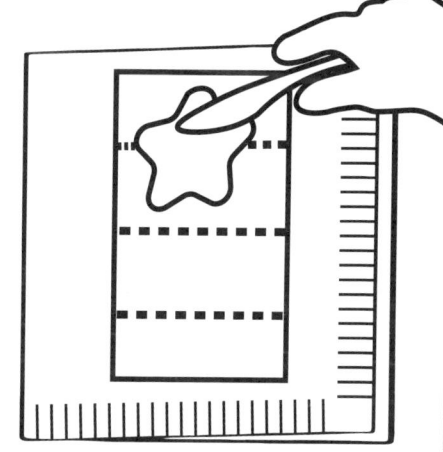

Spread topping on the graham cracker

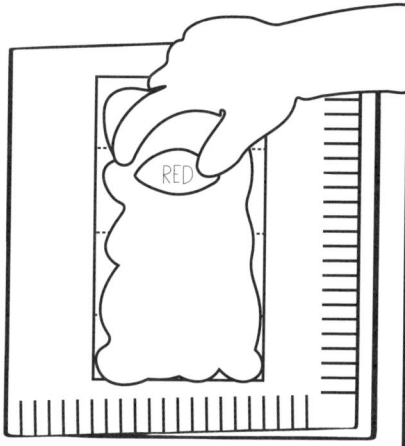

Place the red apple slice on the top

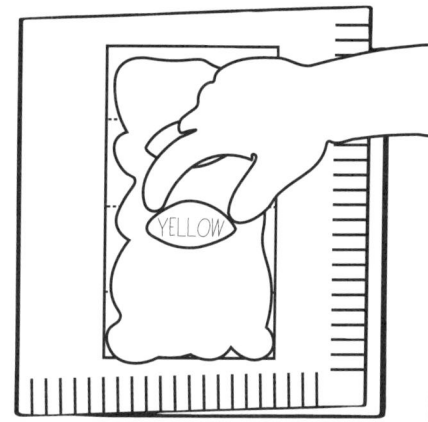

Place the yellow apple slice in the middle

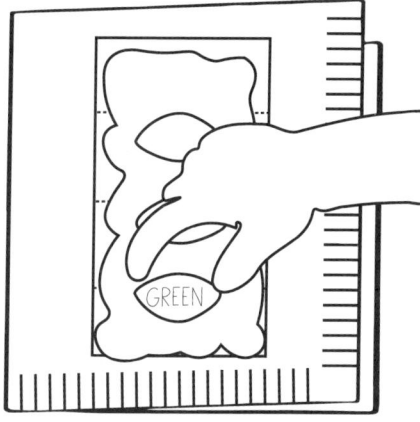

Place the green apple slice on the bottom

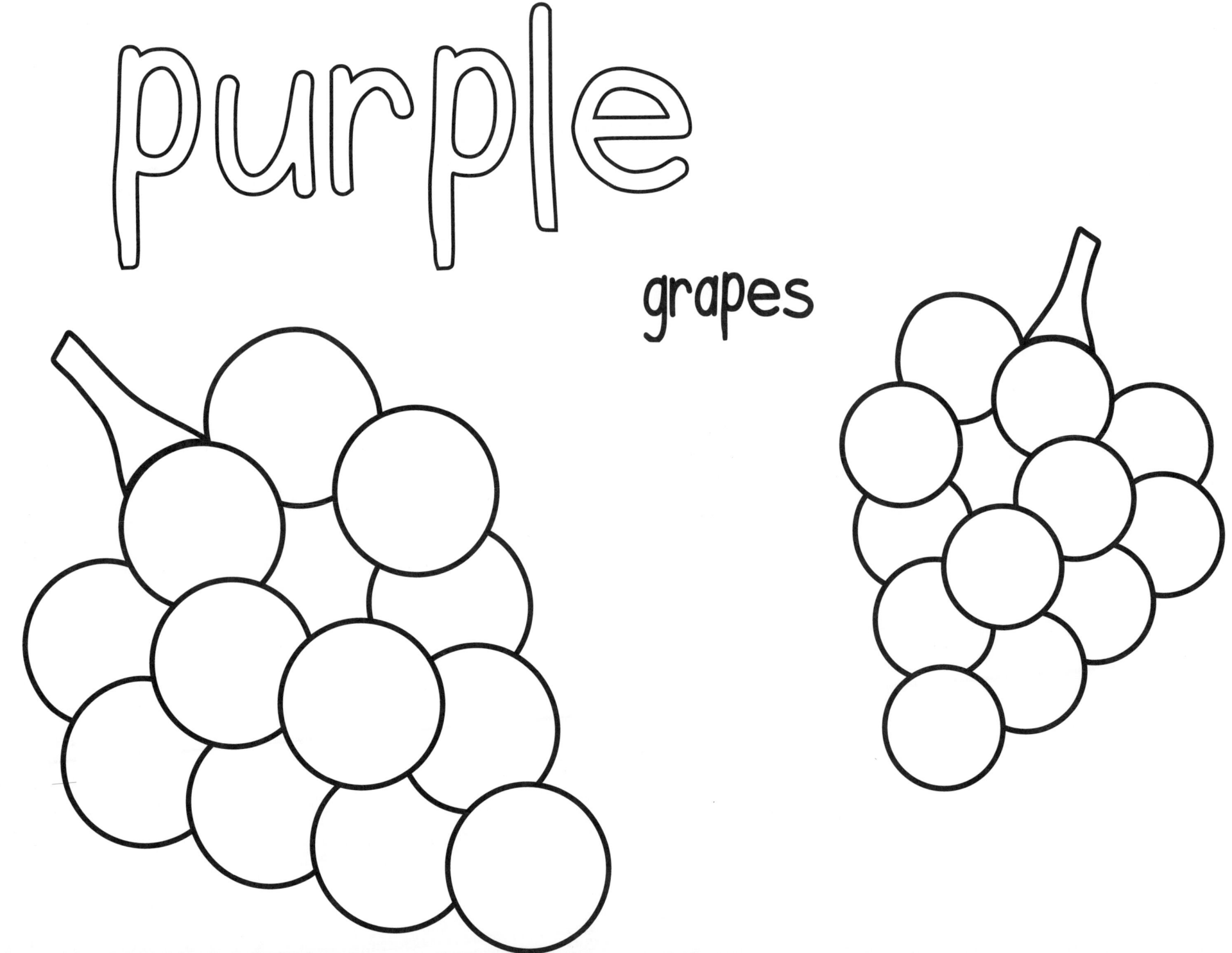

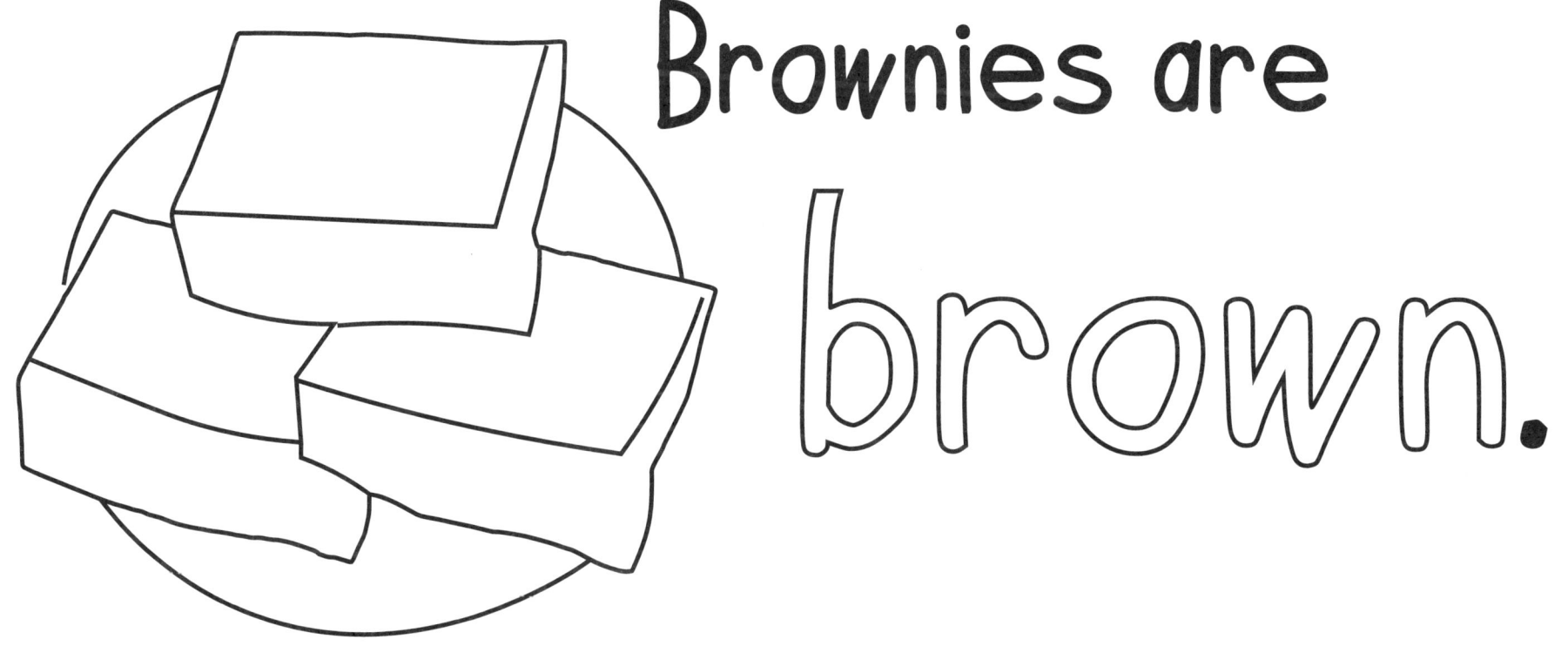

black bats

black hat

Use your crayons to color these with colors you like!

My favorite color is

_____.

Aa Bb Cc Dd Ee Ff Gg Hh Ii Jj Kk Ll Mm

The alphabet goes from A to Z. Learning letters is fun to me.

Nn Oo Pp Qq Rr Ss Tt Uu Vv Ww Xx Yy Zz

Say it	Color it
Aa	Aa

Trace it	Write it
Aa	

Say it

B b

Color it

B b

Trace it

B b

Write it

Say it

C c

Color it

C c

Trace it

C c

Write it

Say it **D d**	Color it 
Trace it 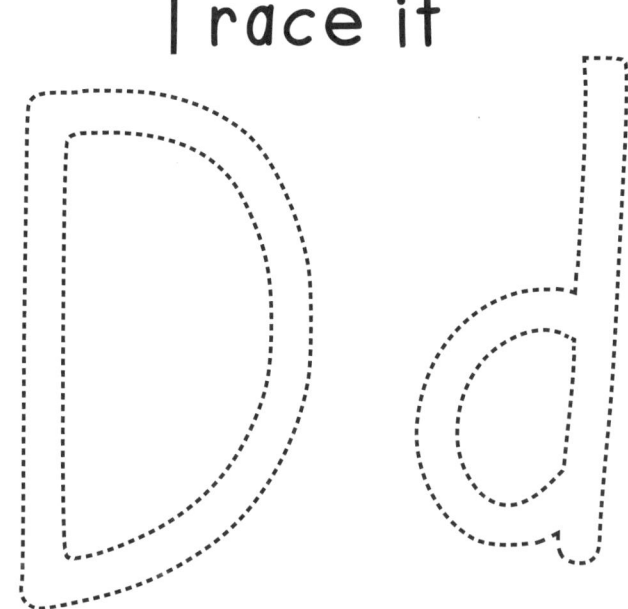	Write it 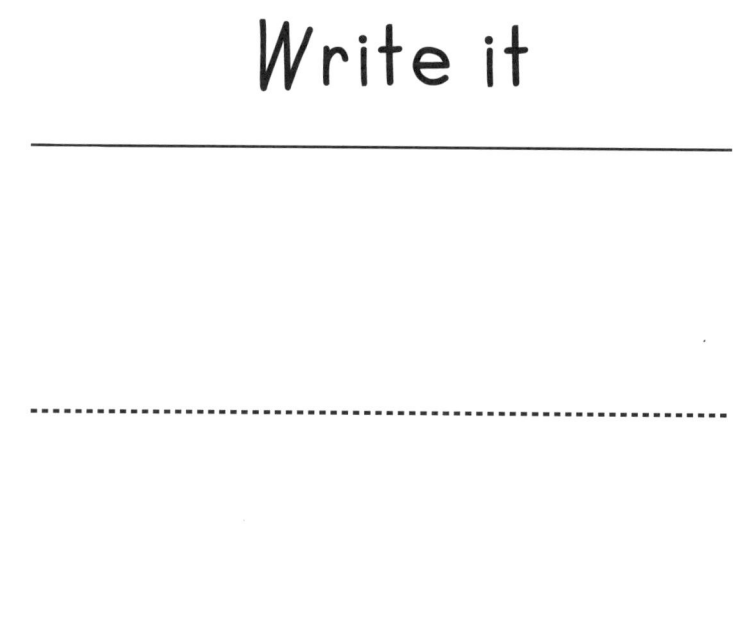

Say it

E e

Color it

E e

Trace it

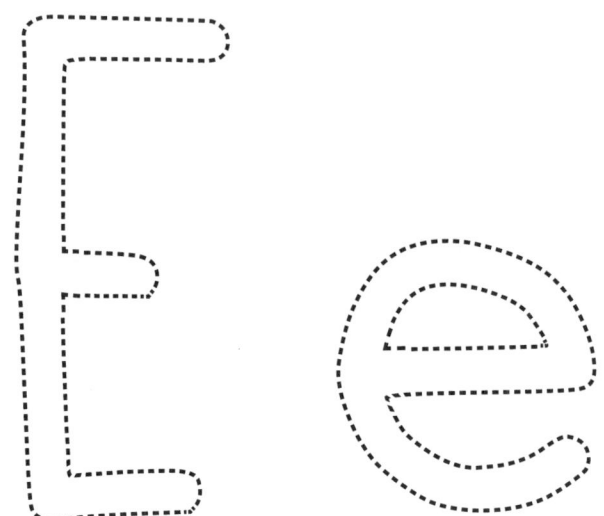

Write it

_____

- - - - - - - - - - -

_____

Say it

G g

Color it

G g

Trace it

G g

Write it

_____   _____

------------   ------------

_____   _____

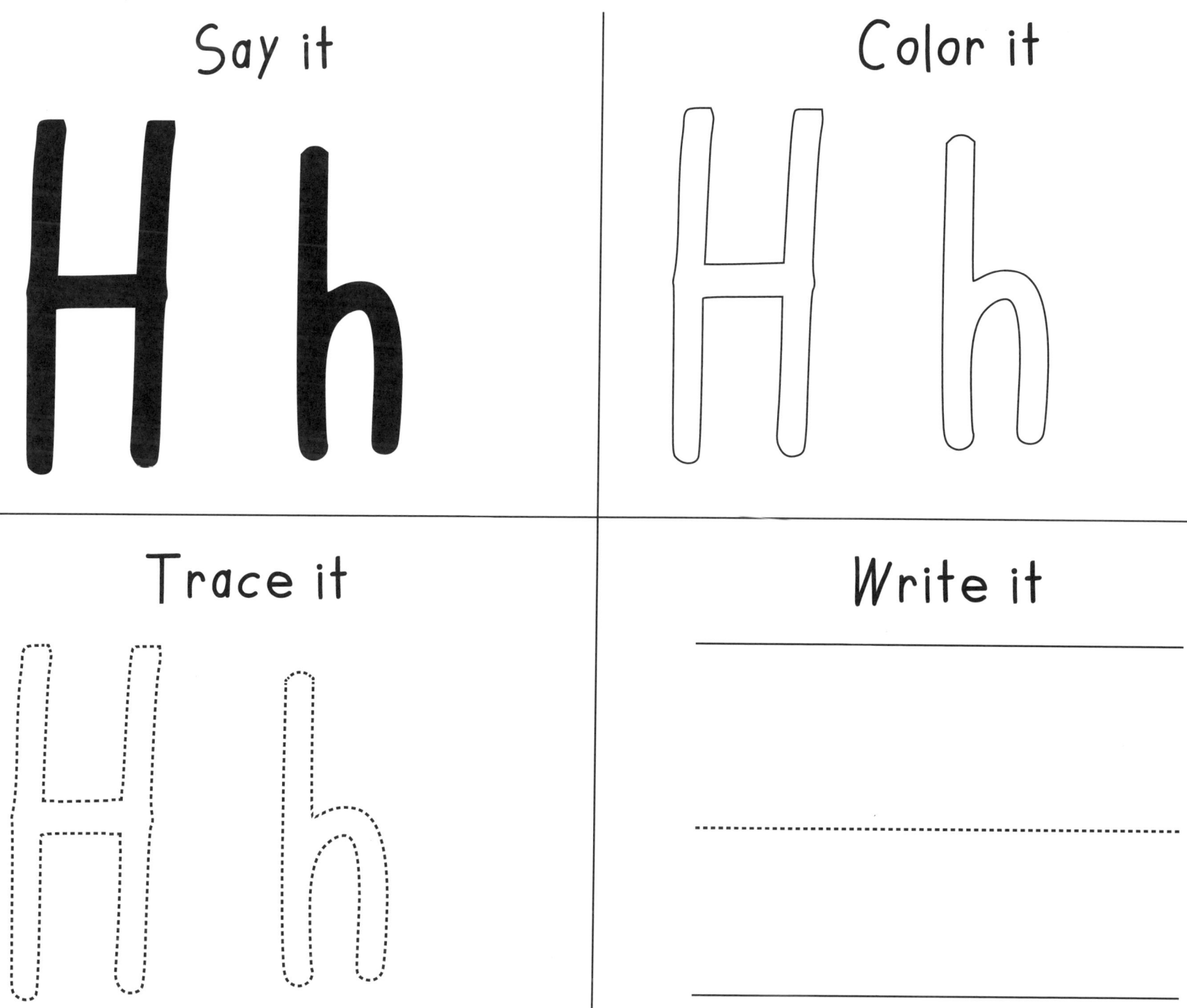

Say it

I i

Color it

I i

Trace it

I i

Write it

Say it

J j

Color it

J j

jelly

Trace it

J j

Write it

Say it

K k

Color it

K k

Trace it

K k

Write it

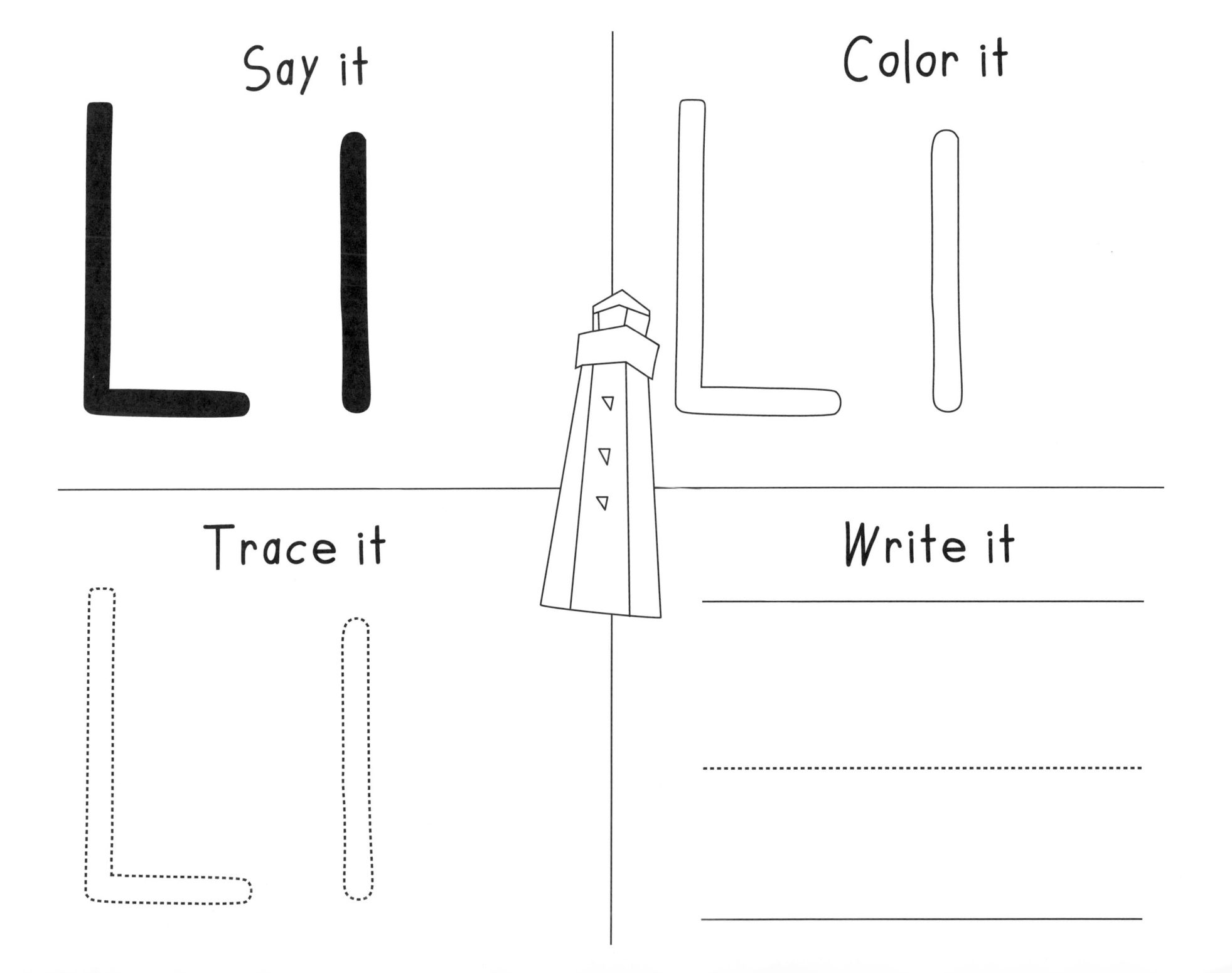

Say it

Color it

Trace it

Write it

Say it

M m

Color it

M m

Trace it

M m

Write it

Say it

N n

Color it

N n

Trace it

N n

Write it

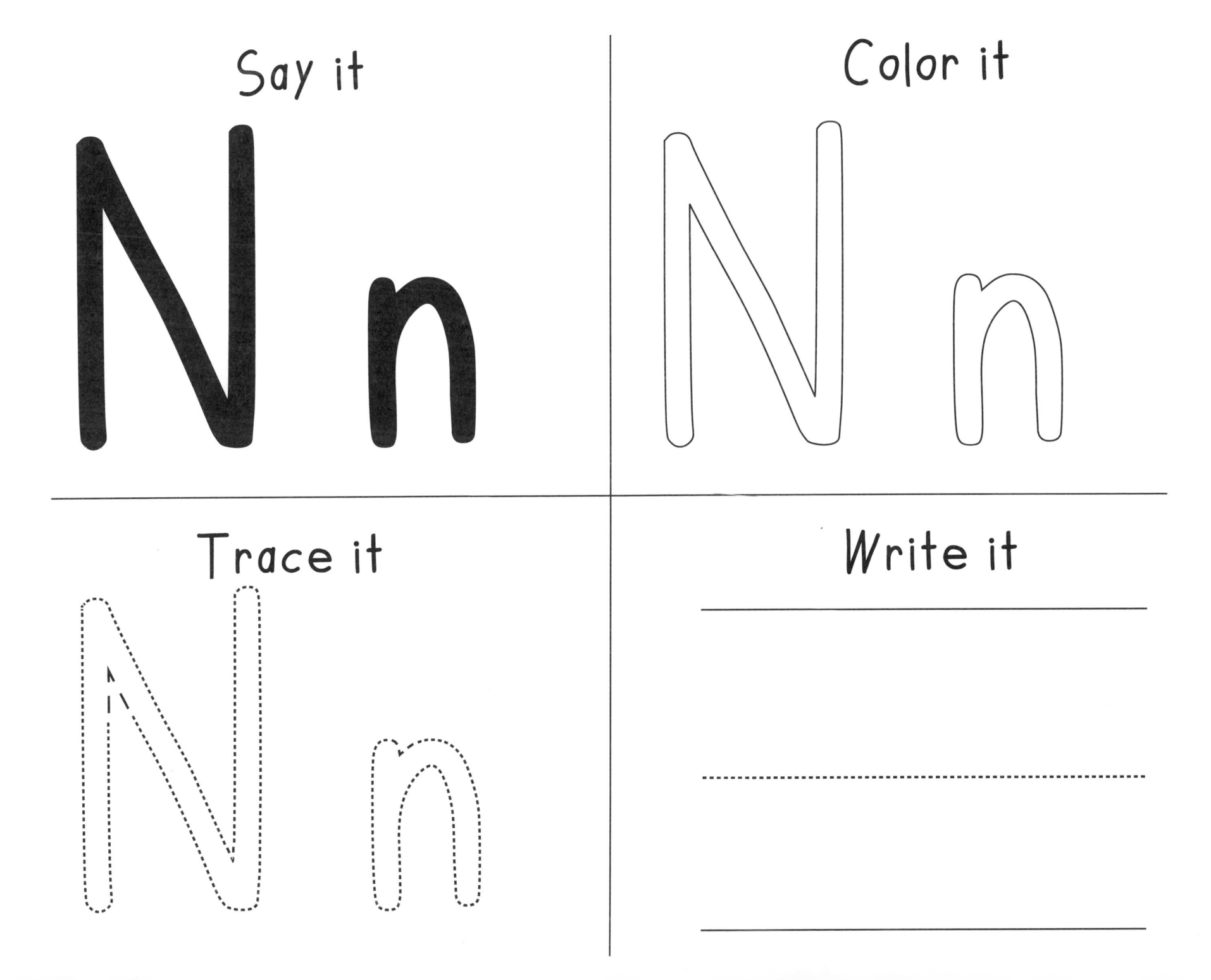

Say it

O o

Color it

Trace it

Write it

Say it

P p

Color it

P p

Trace it

P p

Write it

Say it

Q q

Color it

Q q

Trace it

Q q

Write it

Say it

R r

Color it

R r

Trace it

R r

Write it

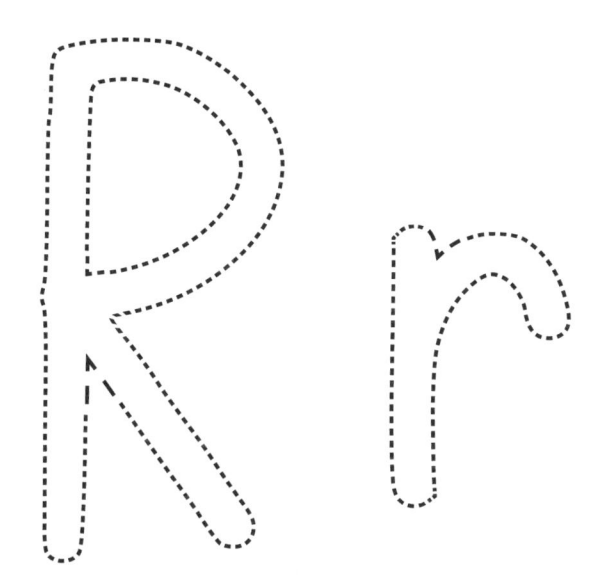

Say it

S s

Color it

S s

STOP

Trace it

S s

Write it

Say it

T t

Color it

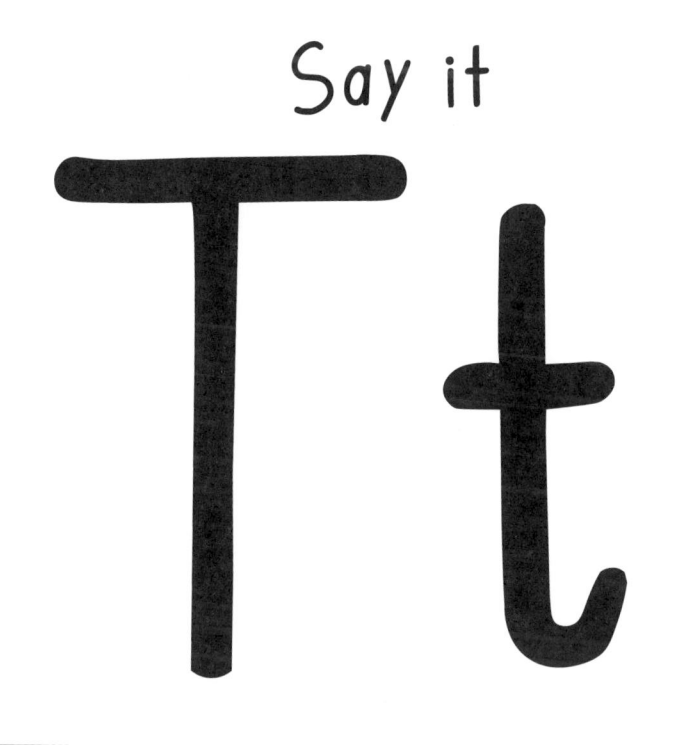

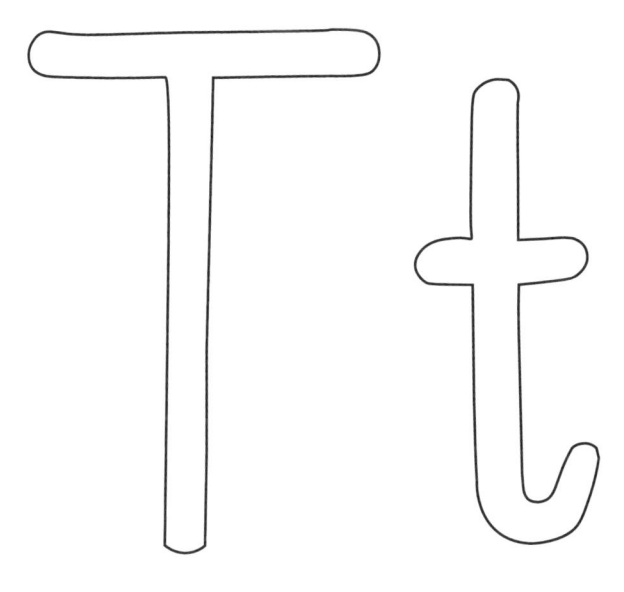

T t

Trace it

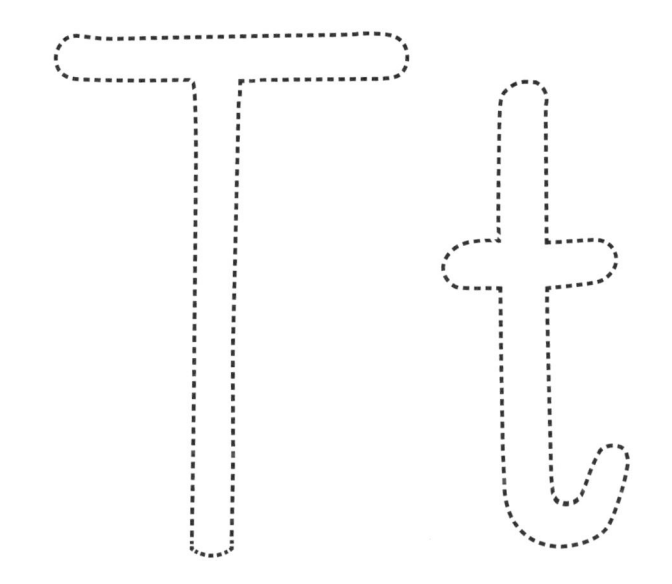

T t

Write it

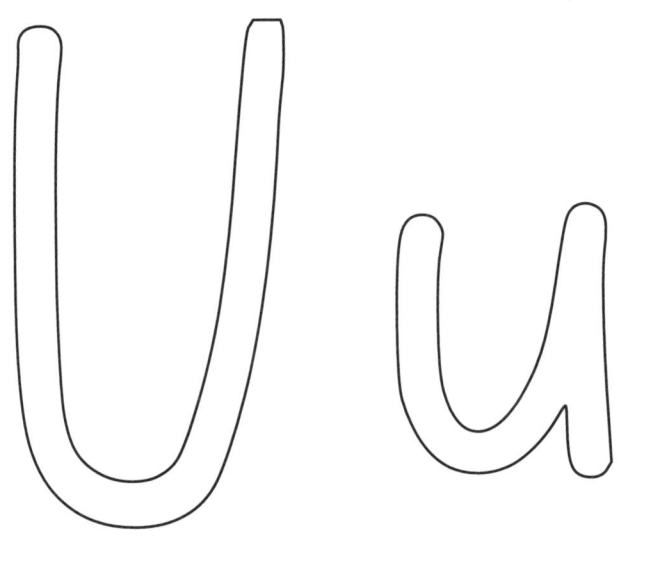

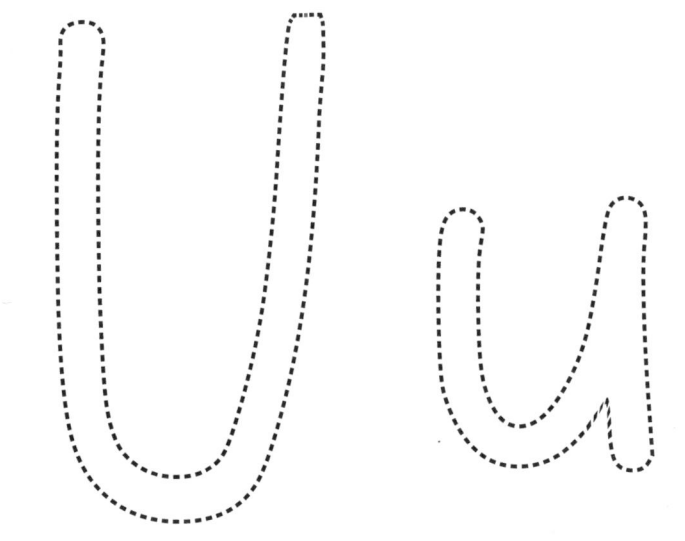

Say it	Color it
Uu	Uu

Trace it	Write it
Uu	

Say it

Vv

Color it

Vv

Trace it

Vv

Write it

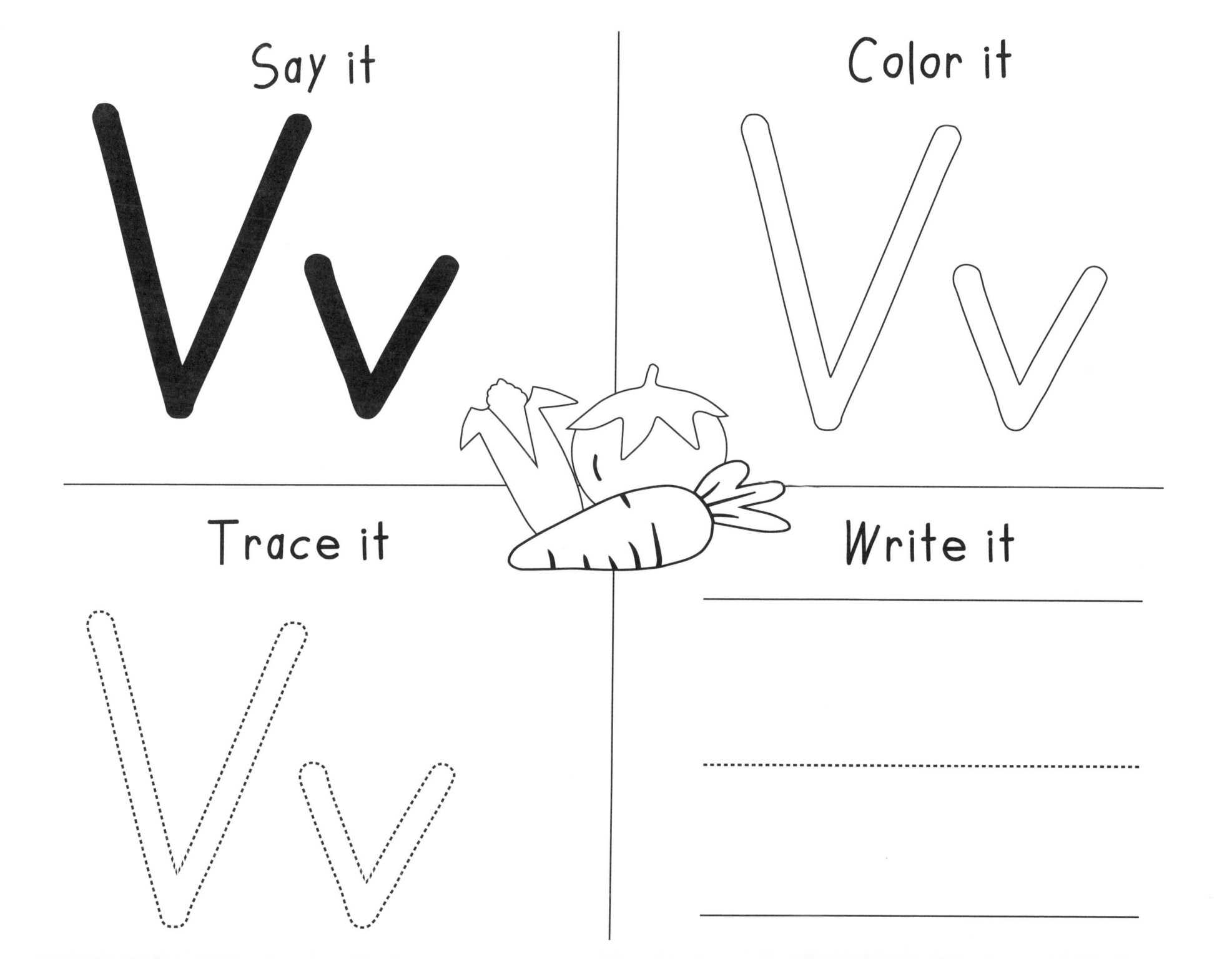

Say it

Ww

Color it

Trace it

Write it

Say it X x	Color it X x
Trace it X x	Write it

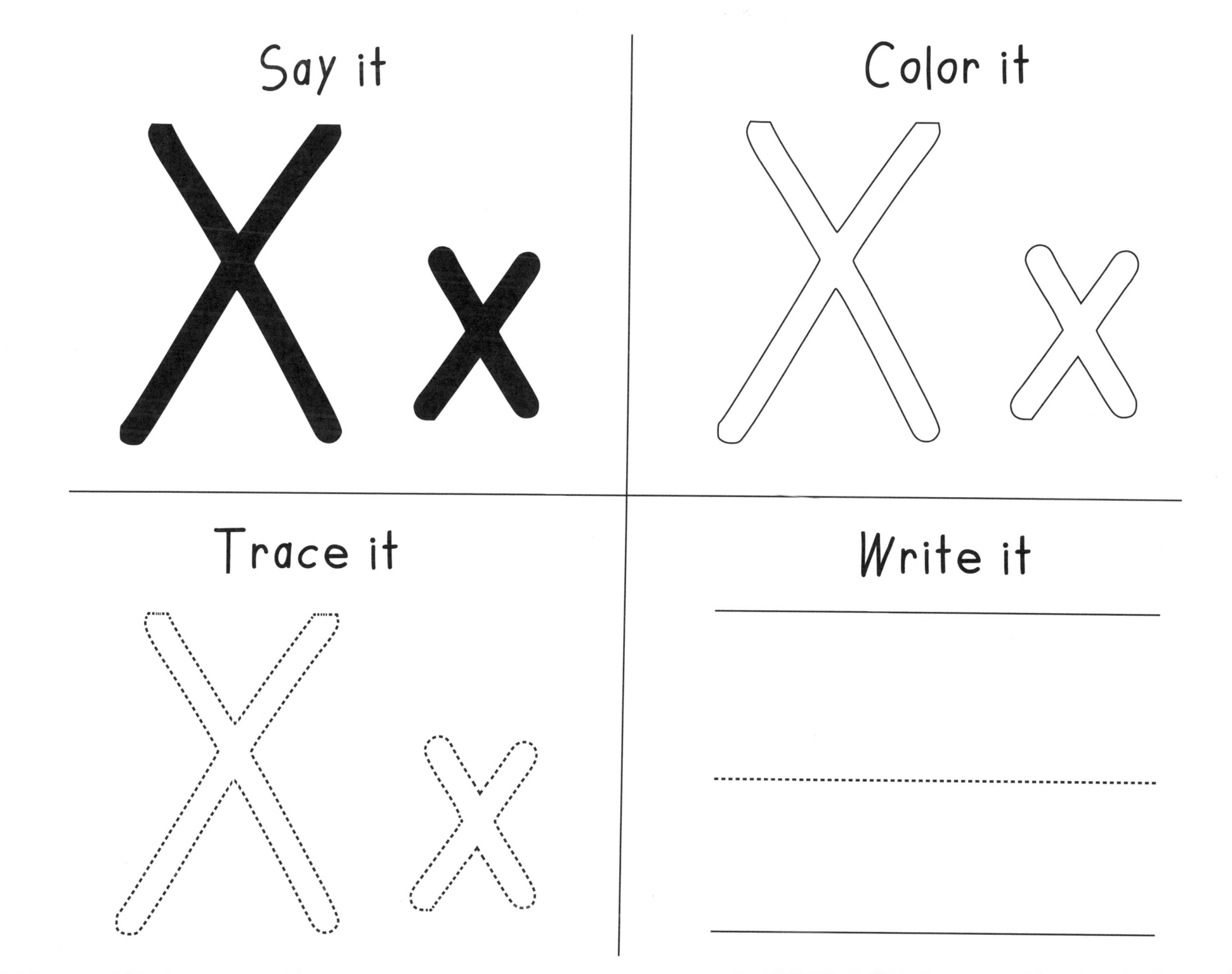

Say it

Color it

Y y

Trace it

Write it

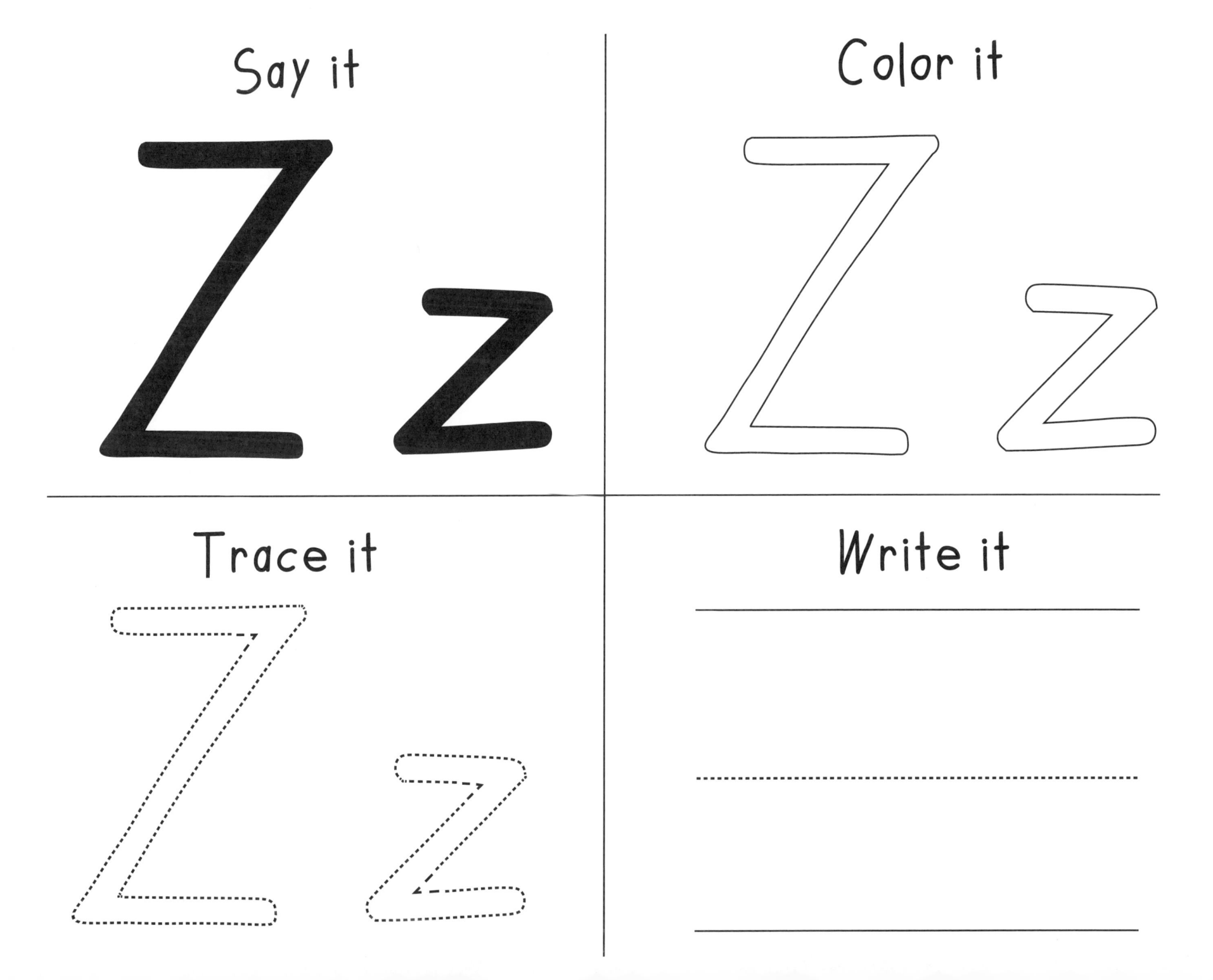

Say it	Color it
Z z	Z z

Trace it	Write it
Z z	

Hands are for helping!　　　　　Trace yours here.

left hand　　　　　　　　　　　　　　　　right hand